Theory Paper   Grade 5   2015   A
Model Answers

1 (a) (i)  (2)

(ii) prominent / make the melody stand out (2)

(iii) (2)

or   or

or   or

(b) (i) Chord A   V 3rd / Vb (2)
Chord B   I 5th / Ic (2)
Chord C   II root / IIa (2)

(ii) (3)

2 1   major 6th (10)
2   perfect 5th
3   augmented 4th
4   minor 10th / compound minor 3rd
5   diminished 7th

3  (10)

or

or

4   *Source: Elgar, 'In the Dawn', Op. 41 No. 1*

(a)   (i)   *All possible answers are shown on the extract reproduced below. For full marks candidates need to identify only one example of each answer.*

       B   Bar 5   (2)
       C   Bar 6 / 8   (2)
       D   Bar 6   (2)

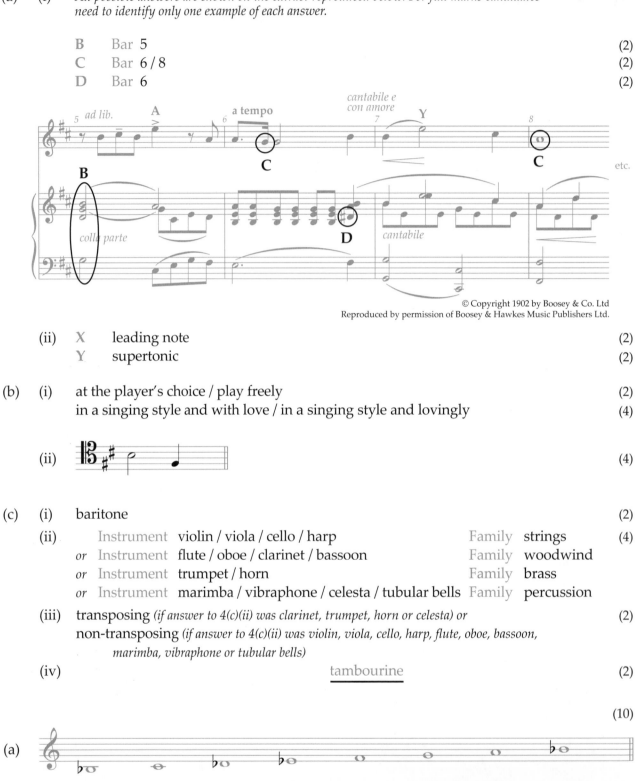

    (ii)   X   leading note   (2)
            Y   supertonic   (2)

(b)   (i)   at the player's choice / play freely   (2)
           in a singing style and with love / in a singing style and lovingly   (4)

    (ii)   (4)

(c)   (i)   baritone   (2)

	Instrument	Family	
	violin / viola / cello / harp	strings	(4)
or	flute / oboe / clarinet / bassoon	woodwind	
or	trumpet / horn	brass	
or	marimba / vibraphone / celesta / tubular bells	percussion	

    (iii)   transposing *(if answer to 4(c)(ii) was clarinet, trumpet, horn or celesta)* or   (2)
            non-transposing *(if answer to 4(c)(ii) was violin, viola, cello, harp, flute, oboe, bassoon, marimba, vibraphone or tubular bells)*

    (iv)   tambourine   (2)

5   (10)

6 *There are many ways of completing this question. Either of the specimen completions below would receive full marks.* (15)

EITHER

(a) cello

OR

The jol - ly god in tri - umph comes; Sound_ the trum-pets, beat the drums!

7 (10)

EITHER

(a) Chord A   IV / B♭ major   Chord C   II / G minor
     Chord B   I / F major   Chord D   I / F major
                                   Chord E   V / C major

OR

(b)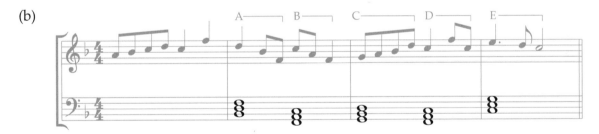

Theory Paper   Grade 5   2015   B
Model Answers

1 (a) compound (1)
          quadruple (1)

   (b) 1   augmented 11th / compound augmented 4th (2)
        2   minor 6th (2)
        3   major 7th (2)

   (c) B♭ major (2)

(d)   on the G string   (2)

(e)    (3)

2   (10)

etc.

3   *Source: T. Kullak, 'Vögelchens Tod', No. 9 from Kleine Stücke, Op. 62*

(a)   (i)   sweet / gentle   (2)
              sad / sorrowful   (2)
              forced / forcing / accented   (2)

      (ii)      (4)

(b)   (i)   Chord X   V 5th / Vc   (2)
              Chord Y   I 3rd / Ib   (2)
      (ii)   **A**   dominant   (2)
              B   mediant   (2)

      (iii)   (2)

              or

              or

(c)   (i)   C minor   (2)
      (ii)   flute / oboe / clarinet   (2)
      (iii)   Family   strings   Instrument   double bass / bass / harp   (4)
              or Family   brass   Instrument   tuba / bass tuba
              or Family   percussion   Instrument   timpani / kettledrums

      (iv)   false   (2)

4   (10)

(a)

(b)

5 (10)

6 *There are many ways of completing this question. Either of the specimen completions below would receive full marks.* (15)

EITHER

(a) trumpet

OR

7 (10)

EITHER

(a) Chord A V / G major   Chord C II / D minor
    Chord B I / C major   Chord D V / G major
                               Chord E I / C major

OR

(b)

Model Answers

1   (a)   (i)   Bar 1:    Bar 4:   Bar 5:   (6)

     (ii)   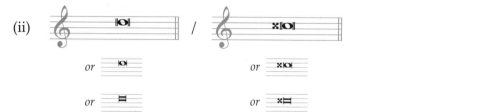   (2)

   (b)   (i)   Chord A   IV root / IVa   (2)
              Chord B   I 5th / Ic   (2)

     (ii)   (3)

2   1   perfect 11th / compound perfect 4th   (10)
    2   augmented 4th
    3   major 6th
    4   minor 7th
    5   diminished 5th

3      (10)

4   *Source: Fauré, Sicilienne, Op. 78*

   (a)   (i)   50 dotted crotchets in a minute / 50 dotted quarter notes in a minute /   (2)
                    50 dotted crotchet beats in a minute / 50 dotted quarter-note beats in a minute
              with the bow / bowed   (2)
              always / ever   (2)

     (ii)   (4)

(b) (i)   *There are two possible answers to this question. Either of the brackets shown on the extract reproduced above would receive full marks.* (2)

(ii) *There are two possible answers to this question. Either of the circles shown on the extract reproduced above would receive full marks.* (2)

(iii) melodic (2)

(iv) **A**   mediant (2)
     B   leading note (2)

(c) (i)   true (2)
        false (2)

(ii) <u>bassoon</u> (2)

(iii) Family woodwind   Instrument flute / piccolo (4)
    or Family brass   Instrument trumpet
    or Family percussion Instrument glockenspiel / xylophone / celesta

9

5 (10)

(a)

(b)

6 *There are many ways of completing this question. Either of the specimen completions below would receive full marks.* (15)

EITHER

(a) violin

OR

(b)

Lo! I am come to___ au - tumn, When all___ the leaves are gold.

7 (10)

EITHER

(a) Chord A II / A minor Chord D IV / C major
    Chord B I / G major Chord E I / G major
    Chord C V / D major

OR

(b)
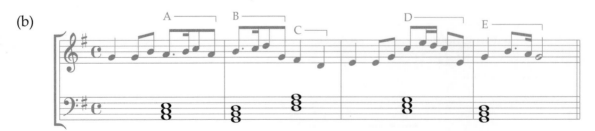

1 **(a)** **(i)** **A**   lower mordent / inverted mordent / mordent (2)

   B   appoggiatura / leaning note (2)

   (ii)   demisemiquaver / 32nd note (2)

   (iii) **X**   leading note (2)

   Y   submediant (2)

(b) **(i)**  etc. (3)

or (from image)

   (ii)   simple (1)

   triple (1)

2 1   augmented 4th (10)

   2   major 6th

   3   perfect 11th / compound perfect 4th

   4   diminished 5th

   5   minor 7th

3 (10)

4   *Source: Reger, 'Ach, Baümchen, du stehst grüne', No. 2 from Acht Ausgewählte Volkslieder für gemischten Chor, WoO VI/11.*

   (a) **(i)**   with expression / expressively (4)

   more (2)

   (ii)   D minor (2)

   (iii)   *The answer is shown by the square bracket on the extract reproduced below.* (2)

11

(b)　(i)　Chord X　II 3rd / IIb　　　　　　　　　　　　　(2)
　　　　　　Chord Y　IV root / IVa　　　　　　　　　　　　(2)
　　　　　　Chord Z　I 5th / Ic　　　　　　　　　　　　　　(2)

　　(ii)　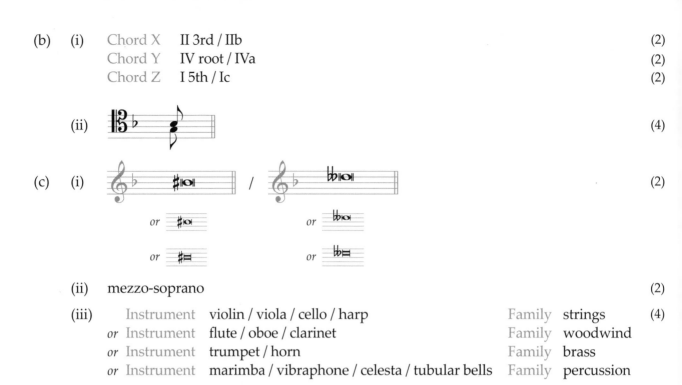　　　　　　　　　　　　　　　　　　　　(4)

(c)　(i)　　　　　　　　　/　　　　　　　　　　　　　　　(2)

　　　　or　　　　　　　　　or

　　　　or　　　　　　　　　or

　　(ii)　mezzo-soprano　　　　　　　　　　　　　　　　(2)

　　(iii)　Instrument　violin / viola / cello / harp　　　　　　Family　strings　(4)
　　　or　Instrument　flute / oboe / clarinet　　　　　　　　Family　woodwind
　　　or　Instrument　trumpet / horn　　　　　　　　　　　Family　brass
　　　or　Instrument　marimba / vibraphone / celesta / tubular bells　Family　percussion

　　(iv)　transposing *(if answer to 4(c)(iii) was clarinet, trumpet, horn or celesta) or*　(2)
　　　　　non-transposing *(if answer to 4(c)(iii) was violin, viola, cello, harp, flute, oboe, marimba or vibraphone)*

5　　　　　　　　　　　　　　　　　　　　　　　　　　(10)

(a)

　　　or

　　　or

(b)

6　*There are many ways of completing this question. Either of the specimen completions below would receive full marks.*　(15)

EITHER

(a)　violin

OR

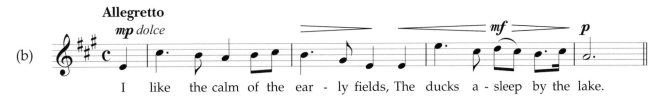

(b)

I like the calm of the ear - ly fields, The ducks a - sleep by the lake.

7   (10)

EITHER

(a)   Chord A   IV / G major   Chord D   II / E minor
       Chord B   V / A major   Chord E   V / A major
       Chord C   I / D major

OR

(b)

13